WHERE SHOULD I GO IN EGYPT?

GEOGRAPHY 4TH GRADE
CHILDREN'S AFRICA BOOKS

Speedy Publishing LLC

40 E. Main St. #1156

Newark, DE 19711

www.speedypublishing.com

Copyright 2017

One of our oldest continuous civilizations has its home along the banks of the Nile River in Egypt. If you could visit Egypt today, what should you go see? Let's take a look!

THE LONG CULTURE OF EGYPT

The story of civilization in Egypt starts over five thousand years ago. The rich land along the Nile River supported a rich and powerful civilization. Cities grew up and the people of the land grew enough to support a vast population.

The Egyptian people developed writing, mathematics, surveying, military skills, and a complex religion. The Pharaoh, the king of the nation, was also the head of its religion.

PHAROAH

EGYPTIAN TOMB

Egyptian people believed in a life after this life, and buried important people with images of the goods they would need in the next life. They also embalmed the bodies of pharaohs and other leaders, preserving their bodies for the passage to the next life. Learn about their treatment of important bodies in the Baby Professor book *How are Mummies Made?*

The great Egyptian empire began to weaken about three thousand years ago. It was conquered by other peoples several times: by the Assyrians, the Persians, and the Greeks. Finally, in 30 BCE, Egypt became part of the Roman Empire. In 642 CE, Islamic armies conquered Roman Egypt, and from then on the history of Egypt is as part of the Muslim world. Learn more in the Baby Professor book What is Islam?

Each of these cultures left its mark on Egypt, and you can see monuments, tombs, and great buildings from the distant and recent past.

ABU SIMBEL TEMPLE

CHURCH

THE START OF TOURISM TO EGYPT

People have been visiting Egypt as tourists since early in the Roman Empire. They traveled to see the wonders of the world, and to bring home souvenirs and works of art from distant places. But you can see today a lot of things that ancient Roman tourists could not see: even great sites like the pyramids were buried under sand for hundreds or even thousands of years, and were only made available to visit again in the last two hundred years.

WHERE TO GO IN THE CITIES

Egypt is home to many millions of people, and its cities are great and complex. Here are just a few highlights of what you can see there:

Cairo

Cairo, the capital of Egypt, was built near the site of the ancient capital, Memphis. It has layers and layers of history!

NILE RIVER

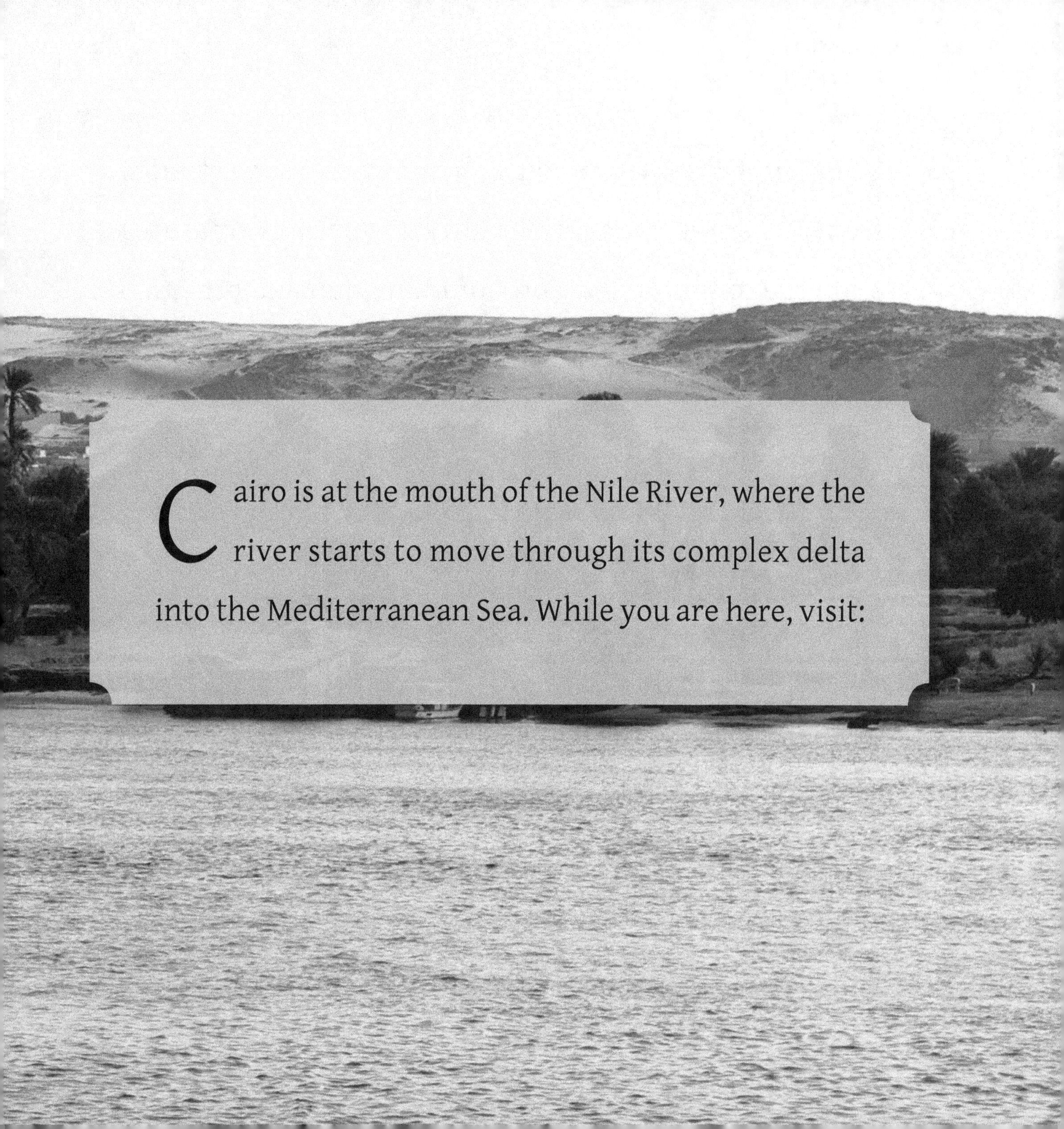
Cairo is at the mouth of the Nile River, where the river starts to move through its complex delta into the Mediterranean Sea. While you are here, visit:

- **The Egyptian Museum** at Tahrir Square: see artifacts from all periods of Egyptian culture, especially treasures from the tombs of Pharaoh Tutankhamun and others.

○ **The Pyramids of Giza** are just a short trip outside of Cairo. They are dramatic burial sites, and impressive from certain angles, as long as you can ignore the endless souvenir shops and food stalls near them.

- **The Nile at night**: take a ride on the Nile in a felucca, a traditional river boat, to see the city at its best and most romantic.

- **Khan El-Khalili** is an Islamic neighborhood with houses almost seven hundred years old. There are winding streets, and little shops where you can find authentic Egyptian goods that are not like what the tourist shops sell. The people in the neighborhood are very welcoming to visitors.

Al-Jama's Al-Anwar is the "Enlightened Mosque". It was built over one thousand years ago and is named after an early caliph, or ruler. It is both a well-used place of worship and a quiet retreat from the noise and confusion of the city.

- **The Al-Azhar Mosque** was the place where one of the oldest universities in the world began. Students study science, mathematics, literature and many other topics, along with the teachings of Islam.

- **Sultan Qalaun Mosque** was built in the eight century, and includes architectural styles brought from Moorish Spain and from the churches of medieval Europe.

ALEXANDRIA

Alexandria was one of the great cities of the ancient world. It was Egypt's main port on the Caribbean after Alexander the Great founded

in 331 BCE, and was home to one of the most famous libraries of human history. Its lighthouse, the Pharos, was one of the Seven Wonders of the World.

ALEXANDRIA'S WATERFRONT

Most of ancient Alexandria is lost to us now, partly because of earthquakes and wars and partly because it has sunk under the Mediterranean. It is still worth a visit because of the museums of artifacts and its views of the sea.

Aswan

Far to the south along the Nile River is Aswan, on the shore of Lake Nasser. The lake was created when Egypt build the Aswan Dam, providing electrical power to the nation. The city is a good base for visiting ancient and modern wonders like the Temple of Philae and the Sun Temple of Pharaoh Ramses II. Both of these ancient buildings had to be taken apart and rebuilt on higher ground to be preserved from the rising waters building up behind the Aswan Dam.

AGA KHAN MAUSOLEUM, ASWAN

WHERE TO GO
IN THE COUNTRY

The cities of Egypt are largely in a narrow strip along the fertile Nile River valley. But there are many other wonders to see away from the bright lights! Here are some:

BLUE HOLE BEACH, DAHAB

Dahab

Dahab is an informal resort on the Gulf of Aqaba, at the very south of the Sinai Desert. It is a perfect place for ocean pleasures like scuba diving and wind-surfing, and dry-land adventures like rock climbing and desert travels with local Bedouin guides.

Siwa Oasis

In the west of Egypt, near the border with Libya, Siwa Oasis did not modernize along with the rest of the country until very recently. To visit the oasis is to get a sense of how the people of Egypt lived hundreds of years ago, and how central to that life sources of fresh water were. There are ancient ruins of mud forts, and buildings from the Greek and Roman periods of Egyptian history.

OLD TOWN OF SHALI IN SIWA OASIS

Sharm el-Sheikh

Sharm el-Sheikh is a beach resort on the Sinai Peninsula. It is said to have some of the best snorkeling and diving sites in the world. There are

also day trips to places like The Colored Canyon, Mount Sinai (where Moses received the Ten Commandments from God), and an ancient Christian community, St. Catherine's Monastery.

RED PYRAMID

Dahshur

The major tomb and pyramid sites of Egypt, like Luxor and Giza, can be overcrowded with visitors and people selling things to tourists. Hahshur, not far from Cairo, is a smaller and more peaceful example of the traditional Egyptian way of honoring the dead. The Bent Pyramid is here, as is the Red Pyramid, which is almost five thousand years old!

The White Desert

The White Desert looks like somewhere on another planet. It has notable rock formations, and is a popular place for overnight camping trips.

Whale Valley

In Fayoum is Wadi El-Hitan, or "Whale Valley". Archaeologists have found here hundreds of fossils of archaeoceti, the ancestors of all the whales. It is also a great place for star-gazing, as the valley is far from any light-producing city or industrial area.

Desert Breath

Near Hurghada, on the edge of the Red Sea, is an art installation called Desert Breath. It was created in 1997 by three artists, and is made of dozens of tall cones of earth forming a double spiral. At the center of the installation is a large pool of water. You can see the installation from the International Space Station, if you happen to be visiting there, as it covers about 100,000 square meters!

DESERT BREATH

The installation is designed to gradually erode back into its surroundings, and eventually it will disappear. But for now it is well worth a visit.

DESERT BREATH

WHAT NOT TO DO

Don't ride a camel around the pyramids. Instead, see the pyramids on foot to save money, and for your camel experience hire a guide to take you on a trip into the desert. Go out at sunset and enjoy the sandy expanse as the day cools down and the evening stars start to appear.

VALLEY OF THE KINGS

Don't take a tour of the tombs at Luxor. The great artifacts found in those tombs are not in Luxor any more, but in museums in Cairo and other places. Instead, visit tombs in quieter places like Dahshur. In the Valley of the Kings, instead of visiting the tomb of King Tut, visit the less-well-known tomb of Ramses V. The walls are painted in surprisingly bright colors.

Don't climb Mount Sinai to see the sun rise. A lot of people climb this mountain for the start of the day, making it a crowded event. Also, the path is tricky in the dark of late night. Instead, climb the mountain at the end of the day, enjoy a meal as the sun sets and the stars come out—and then camp out overnight! You will have a wonderful wilderness experience, and if you want to see the sunrise you will already be in place before other tourists start to arrive.

SUNRISE ON MOUNT SINAI

YOUR NEXT TRIP

After you have seen some of the wonders of Egypt, where will you go next? Get some ideas from Baby Professor books like *Who Built the Great Wall of China?*, *Places to See and People to Meet in Ireland*, and *Let's Go to España!*

THE GREAT WALL OF CHINA

Visit
BABY PROFESSOR
EDUCATION KIDS
www.BabyProfessorBooks.com
to download Free Baby Professor eBooks
and view our catalog of new and exciting
Children's Books